PANDEMICS:
COVID-19 AND OTHER GLOBAL HEALTH THREATS

Jill Keppeler

ROSEN
PUBLISHING

NEW YORK

Published in 2022 by The Rosen Publishing Group, Inc.
29 East 21st Street, New York, NY 10010

Copyright © 2022 by The Rosen Publishing Group, Inc.

First Edition

All rights reserved. No part of this book may be reproduced in any form without permission in writing from the publisher, except by a reviewer.

Editor: Greg Roza
Book Design: Michael Flynn

Photo Credits: Cover skaman306/Moment/Getty Images; (series globe background) photastic/Shutterstock.com; p. 4 Radoslav Zilinsky/Moment/Getty Images; p. 5 izusek/E+/Getty Images; p. 7 ePhotocorp/iStock/Getty Images; p. 8 DEA/G. DAGLI ORTI/De Agostini Picture Library/Getty Images; p. 9 Time Life Pictures/The LIFE Picture Collection/ Getty Images; p. 11 Stock Montage/Archive Photos/Getty Images; p. 13 Anthony Kwan/Getty Images; p. 14 RichVintage/E+/Getty Images; p. 15 Frederic J. Brown/AFP/Getty Images; p. 17 Pier Marco Tacca/Getty Images; p. 18 Anadolu Agency/Getty Images; p. 19 Gary Hershorn/Getty Images; p. 21 MediaNews Group/Long Beach Press-Telegram/Getty Images; p. 22 The Washington Post/Getty Images; p. 23 Allen J. Schaben/Los Angeles Times/Getty Images; p. 25 damircudic/E+/Getty Images; p. 26 picture alliance/Getty Images; p. 27 Bloomberg/Getty Images; p. 29 Newsday LLC/Newsday/Getty Images.

Library of Congress Cataloging-in-Publication Data

Names: Keppeler, Jill, author.
Title: Pandemics : COVID-19 and other global health threats / Jill
    Keppeler.
Description: New York : Rosen Publishing, [2022] | Series: Spotlight on
    global issues | Includes index.
Identifiers: LCCN 2022043878 | ISBN 9781499471816 (library binding) | ISBN
    9781499471786 (paperback) | ISBN 9781499471793 (6 pack)
Subjects: LCSH: COVID-19 (Disease)--Juvenile literature. |
    Epidemics--Juvenile literature.
Classification: LCC RA644.C67 K47 2022 | DDC 614.5/92414--dc23
LC record available at https://lccn.loc.gov/2022043878

Manufactured in the United States of America

Some of the images in this book illustrate individuals who are models. The depictions do not imply actual situations or events.

CPSIA Compliance Information: Batch #CSR22 For further information contact Rosen Publishing, New York, New York at 1-800-237-9932.

Find us on

CONTENTS

CHAPTER ONE

A TIME OF SICKNESS

Before 2020, most people probably didn't think much about the chances of a major epidemic or pandemic in their lives. Perhaps they thought those were only things of the past, or they thought that modern medicine would take care of anything quickly. Surely, there was nothing to worry about.

But on December 31, 2019, officials in Wuhan, China, first reported cases of COVID-19, a disease caused by a new coronavirus. This is a type of virus named for the spikes on its surface. These spikes look something like a crown, and "corona" means "crown." Scientists already knew about coronaviruses, but this seemed to be a new one.

COVID-19 VIRUS

The sickness it caused was new, as well. Within just a few days, more than 40 people were infected by it. Within a week, scientists had identified the new virus. And within 11 days after that first report, the first victim died from COVID-19.

That was just the beginning. By October 2020, there were more than a million deaths from COVID-19 around the world, with millions of known cases of the disease. The virus has spread to every continent but Antarctica. Many people have lost their jobs, and global economies have been damaged. Today, we're living in a time unlike any other.

However, by working together and taking precautions, we can beat COVID-19. It's important to know about how viruses work, what scientists know so far about the disease and the virus, and what you can do to stop its spread.

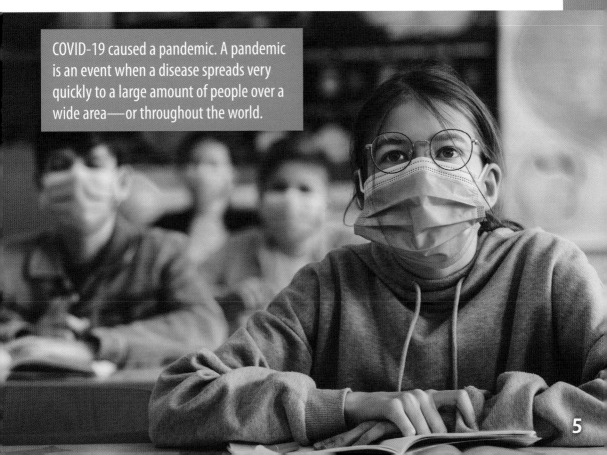

COVID-19 caused a pandemic. A pandemic is an event when a disease spreads very quickly to a large amount of people over a wide area—or throughout the world.

CHAPTER TWO

A VIEW
ON VIRUSES

Viruses are tiny particles, ones that can only be seen with powerful microscopes. They're even smaller than bacteria. Viruses aren't really alive, and they can only grow and reproduce and spread within living cells. They're very simple—but they cause many diseases in humans, including polio, chicken pox, and influenza. A coronavirus also causes the common cold!

Viruses can have many different shapes. Coronaviruses, as mentioned before, are named for their spiky "crown." A kind of coronavirus also causes SARS, which stands for "severe acute respiratory syndrome," in humans. In late 2002, SARS spread from Asia through many parts of the world, causing great worry and a number of quarantines and safety measures. However, the outbreak was controlled by the end of July 2003. More than 8,000 people caught SARS, and fewer than 800 people died from it.

SARS was similar in some ways to COVID-19. Scientists believe that SARS started in a kind of bat or another animal and then jumped to humans. COVID-19 may have done the same. No one's sure where it came from yet, but it may have started in bats and then changed its genes to move to humans. It may also have started with pangolins, a kind of mammal also called a scaly anteater, or other mammals.

The World Health Organization (WHO) has issued guidelines for possible pandemics, including influenza (flu). There are six phases, or levels, from the appearance of a new flu in animals to widespread and continued spread of the flu in humans.

Mammals called civet cats may have been a vector for the SARS virus to pass to humans. Serious diseases often start in animals and jump to humans.

CHAPTER THREE

EPIDEMICS
THROUGH THE YEARS

There have been many epidemics and pandemics throughout the thousands of years of human history, including those caused by illnesses such as cholera, plague, and the flu. The flu is caused by a virus, while cholera and plague are caused by bacteria. A plague hit the Byzantine Empire in the 500s, killing thousands of people. People died so quickly that it was hard to dispose of the bodies fast enough.

However, perhaps the best-known plague is the Black Death, which hit Europe in the 14th century. It may have killed one-fourth to one-third of the population, as many as 25 million people. It was probably spread by fleas and other pests that carried the plague.

In more recent history, the flu pandemic of 1918 to 1919 hit the world (and the United States) hard. Like COVID-19, it spread through people by airborne respiratory droplets. It was called the Spanish flu

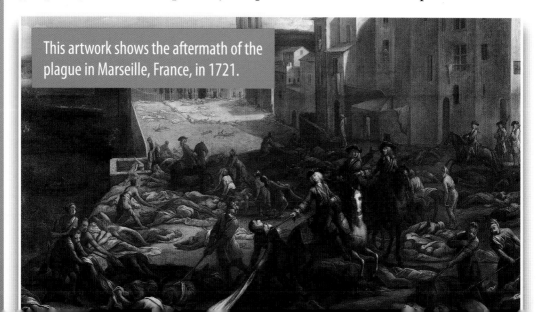

This artwork shows the aftermath of the plague in Marseille, France, in 1721.

because news of the illness first spread from Spain, although it definitely hit other places first. It spread very quickly because this was the time of World War I, which meant there were many soldiers close together, and no pandemic plans existed yet. Millions of people—perhaps up to 100 million—died.

The AIDS epidemic, caused by HIV, arose in the 1980s and killed many people, although there is now a treatment for it. MERS (Middle East respiratory syndrome), also caused by a coronavirus, hit the world in the 2010s, as did the Ebola virus, which killed many people in Africa during that decade. Still, few people seemed to expect the rise of COVID-19.

There were three waves of the Spanish flu from March 1918 to the spring of 1919. This photo shows Seattle, Washington, policemen in 1918, wearing face masks to protect themselves against the flu.

CHAPTER FOUR

LESSONS LEARNED

For every sickness humanity has dealt with over the years, there have been lessons too. In ancient times, people often looked on epidemics as a god's or gods' judgment on humans. Gradually, they learned more about the science behind disease. In the Middle Ages, people learned to quarantine those with some illnesses so that they wouldn't spread. Study of the plagues led to advances in public sanitation.

As time went on, the idea of public health—the art and science of protecting and improving community health through sanitation, preventative measures, and use of science—began to take shape. In the 18th century, people began to create more institutions such as hospitals to care for the sick. Scientists tried to teach people about how disease works.

When the Industrial Revolution started and city populations grew dramatically, the crowding led to even more health problems. People began creating public health boards to deal with the issues. John Snow, a doctor in London during the mid-1800s, became known as "the father of epidemiology" for his work investigating the start and spread of cholera epidemics. He believed the disease was caused by germs instead of bad air, and he proved it with study and science.

More recent epidemics and pandemics have taught us lessons too. The 1918 Spanish flu pandemic showed scientists and historians that social distancing helped keep the sickness from spreading. Communities in which people isolated themselves did better than ones in which people didn't. People also learned that working together is the best way to fight disease.

Greek doctor Hippocrates connected human diseases and the environment in a book written about 400 BC.

11

CHAPTER FIVE

THE RISE OF COVID-19

While Chinese officials reported the first cases of COVID-19 on December 31, 2019, the sickness likely had been around longer than that. However, doctors didn't know quite what it was yet. It was described as a sort of pneumonia, with symptoms including fever, cough, and shortness of breath.

Epidemiologists looked for the cause, taking samples from people to find out who was sick and doing interviews to find out where they'd been. It turned out that many of the infected people had visited a live animal market in Wuhan, China. Scientists working with the samples discovered the sickness was caused by a new coronavirus.

COVID-19 (short for "coronavirus disease 2019") spread quickly. Some of those suffering from it began to die. Soon, China faced an epidemic. However, scientists still weren't sure how the illness spread. Things were complicated by Wuhan's central location in China and how many ways there are to travel away from there. The illness quickly spread to other locations in China, and by mid-January, there were confirmed cases outside the country.

By January 23, 2020, Chinese officials ordered a lockdown in Wuhan and a few other cities. No one could enter or leave. However, it was too late to contain the spread. On January 30, WHO declared a "public health emergency of global concern" because of COVID-19. Doctors found evidence that the disease could be transmitted from person to person, even if the new person hadn't been to one of the original danger zones.

痛哀悼李文亮醫生

Mourning Dr. Li Wenliang

沉痛哀悼

李文亮醫生

Mourning Dr Li Wenliang

Li Wenliang was a doctor in China who was one of the first to raise the alarm about the new virus. Chinese police made him stop warning people. On February 7, 2020, the doctor died from COVID-19.

CHAPTER SIX

SPREADING
RELENTLESSLY

By the end of January 2020, there were COVID-19 cases in the United States, India, Philippines, Russia, Spain, Sweden, United Kingdom, Australia, Canada, Germany, Japan, Singapore, the United Arab Emirates, Vietnam, and more countries. February 2 marked the first COVID-19 death outside of China, in the Philippines. Over the next month, dozens of other countries would confirm cases.

Scientists studied more about the illness and the virus. Since both were so new, they had nothing but research on other coronaviruses and similar illnesses to start with. At first, no one was sure how the virus spread or when people were contagious. No one was sure about the incubation period, either. In time, scientists discovered that COVID-19's incubation period could be from one to 14 days—compared to only two days for influenza. That means people can spread the virus long before they know they have it. In fact, some people may be able to spread COVID-19 without any symptoms at all. All of this contributed to the quick spread of the disease.

On March 11, WHO announced that the COVID-19 outbreak was officially considered a pandemic. This was because of how fast and how severely the illness spread—and also because of inaction on the parts of some governments. WHO Director-General Dr. Tedros Adhanom Ghebreyesus said that "all countries can still change the course of this pandemic" if they "detect, test, treat, isolate, trace, and mobilize their people in their response." At the time, there were more than 118,000 cases in 114 countries. More than 4,000 people had died.

Scientists learned that COVID-19 is spread from person to person through tiny droplets formed when an infected person sneezes or breathes out. People can breathe in the droplets or pick them up through touch. That's why masks and handwashing are important.

CHAPTER SEVEN

LESSONS
FROM ITALY

Earlier on, few people seemed convinced of how dangerous COVID-19 could be. After the third death from COVID-19 in Italy on February 23, officials closed down many events in the country. However, the virus continued to spread, and by March 8, Italian officials put a number of areas under a strict quarantine.

Still, things continued to get worse. By late March, Italy had nearly 54,000 cases and nearly 5,000 deaths. By the end of the month, the death toll in the country had passed 10,000. There were strict rules on movement there, and all nonessential businesses were closed.

The worst impact of COVID-19 on Italy came after other countries, including China, had managed to contain the virus for the most part. There were a few reasons for that. Few people in Italy thought the pandemic would be a true crisis at first. Countries had to take action very early to make a big difference, but many politicians were reluctant to do that. Also, people didn't listen to experts. Some places didn't enforce the quarantines.

Officials also put safety measures in place gradually instead of all at once. That let the virus get a foothold in Italy and then expand. Many people didn't start following precautions until after the disease spread throughout the country. Other countries had to learn from new information and change their tactics.

By mid-September, more than 283,000 people in Italy had had COVID-19, and more than 35,000 had died from it. However, the United States would surpass those numbers.

This photo from March 31, 2020, shows a man spraying cleaner in Piazza Duomo in Milan, Italy, the capital of the Lombardy region. That region was the hardest hit in Italy.

CHAPTER EIGHT

TO
U.S. SHORES

The first known case of COVID-19 in the United States was confirmed on January 21, 2020. The man, who lived in Washington State, had recently traveled to Wuhan, China. A few weeks later, in California, the first person died of COVID-19 on February 6. (Original reports had the first U.S. death occurring on February 28. Medical examinations later showed otherwise.)

As in Italy, many U.S. officials (and people in general) didn't think COVID-19 was much of a threat at first. On February 26, President Trump said at a press conference, "We're very, very ready for this," continuing, "the risk to the American people remains very low." He said that the flu was worse than COVID-19—although interviews would later show he knew COVID-19 was worse.

However, the virus was already spreading in the United States. New York State reported its first case on March 1. By March 3, there were 100 known cases in the United States. Things were moving quickly, and there was much confusion. Every state dealt with the outbreaks differently. Testing for the virus was uneven and sometimes ineffective. Some states started to close schools to try to stop the spread.

On March 13, President Trump declared a national emergency because of COVID-19. In the same week, the U.S. Centers for Disease Control (CDC) warned against large gatherings. By March 17, all 50 states had cases of the virus. There had been more than 100 known deaths and more than 6,000 cases.

DAZZLING BROADWAY ONE WISH AT A TIME!

EXACTLY WHAT YOU WISH FOR!

Aladdin
THE HIT BROADWAY MUSICAL

FIRE DEPARTMENT CONNECTION

New York's Broadway shut down on March 12, 2020, as part of the state's efforts to control the spread of COVID-19.

CHAPTER NINE

LESSONS FROM
THE STATES

By March 20, 2020, New York City was the center of the COVID-19 outbreak in the United States. More than 15,000 people in the state had the virus, about half the infections in the country. Schools and restaurants were closed, and all employees of nonessential businesses had to start working at home. However, by April 1, the state had more than 83,000 cases and 2,300 deaths, many in New York City.

New York's conditions had become so bad, so fast, in part because the state and city shut down too late to control the rise in infections. California (and the city of San Francisco), on the other hand, shut down when there were far fewer cases there. New York had many people returning from travel to Europe who brought the virus with them. At least one person was a super-spreader as well. There may also have been other factors, such as population wealth, density, and race. African Americans seem to be hit worse by COVID-19, and New York has a significant African American population.

However, as the pandemic stretched on, New York got more of a grip on the issue. By late July, cases there had slowed thanks to the shutdown. California, on the other hand, had reached more cases than New York. When California officials started to reopen in May and lift shelter-in-place orders, many people began to act like the virus was gone. Parties and gatherings allowed it to spread quickly again. As of early October 2020, California had the most COVID-19 cases in the United States.

California had to shut many businesses and events down again after its COVID-19 numbers soared.

COVID-19
BEACHES
CLOSED
UNTIL FURTHER NOTICE

#covid19longbeach
longbeach.gov/covid19

LONGBEACH
HEALTH & HUMAN SERVICES

CHAPTER TEN

FREEDOM, FEAR, AND RESPONSIBILITY

By March 26, 2020, the United States passed China to lead the world in COVID-19 cases. In the next few months, millions of people would lose their jobs because of the necessary lockdowns and closures. And as the outbreaks continued and the toll grew, problems became more apparent.

Some past CDC directors say that the United States went wrong with its COVID-19 reaction in a few different ways. There were previous plans in place to deal with pandemics, but no one used them, and many leaders denied COVID-19 was a threat. Some scientists noted a lack of government trust in science that could have helped the situation. President Trump had openly contradicted Dr. Anthony Fauci, the top U.S. expert on infectious diseases, about the virus.

While the U.S. government issued the original state of emergency, there was little centralized action after that. The states were mostly left to themselves to figure out responses, testing, closures—and later, reopenings. Reopening too soon meant big increases in cases of the illness, although some politicians pushed for reopening to help the economy in an election year.

DR. ANTHONY FAUCI

Also, some people rebelled against wearing face masks and social distancing. These and other issues around the pandemic became politicized—they became about politics instead of about public health. These measures can keep COVID-19 from spreading, but many conservative politicians (including President Trump) suggested that they were against American freedoms. The United States' culture of individualism worked against containment of the virus.

Meanwhile, by April 28, U.S. cases had passed 1 million. About a month later, U.S. deaths from COVID-19 passed 100,000.

Precautions such as masks and social distancing are designed to help all of society, but some people say they have a right to expose themselves and others to COVID-19. They've even held rallies for the right to do so.

CHAPTER ELEVEN

MASK UP!

One aspect of COVID-19 prevention that has caused a great deal of confusion and rebellion has been the use of face masks. At first, many public health officials didn't recommend that people wear masks. In the early months of the pandemic, many medical personnel had trouble getting personal protective equipment (PPE) because of issues with the United States' supply. Officials warned people against hoarding such equipment because it was needed for health-care workers.

However, science-based recommendations can change as the situation changes and scientists learn more. As time went on, it became clear that some people with no or few symptoms could spread the virus. It made sense that they were breathing out tiny, virus-laden particles called aerosols, which can infect other people. Aerosols can hang in the air longer than larger droplets. Scientists who studied aerosols worked to convince officials of this.

Aerosol spread of the virus meant that greater use of masks could keep people from infecting others as well as protect others from breathing these particles in. Also, people could wear simpler cloth masks instead of the ones better saved for health-care workers. By April 2020, the CDC recommended wearing masks when around other people. WHO followed by June. Some states (including New York) began requiring people to wear masks in public or in businesses, and studies suggest that this helped slow the spread in those places.

Wearing a mask was a simple way for people to help protect others around them and be part of the fight against the COVID-19 pandemic. Still, some people continued to ignore mask requirements.

Masks must be worn over the nose and mouth to be effective in stopping the transmission of airborne diseases.

CHAPTER TWELVE

SYMPTOMS,
TREATMENTS, AND HOPE

Scientists soon discovered that many people who get COVID-19 will only have minor to moderate symptoms. Common symptoms are a fever and chills, a cough, difficulty breathing, tiredness, body aches, or other cold-like signs. However, some people have no symptoms at all. And on the other side, some people will get very ill and need hospitalization, sometimes with a ventilator. Some people—especially older adults or people with underlying health conditions such as heart disease—have died from the illness. Victims have ranged from children to the elderly.

DRIVE-THROUGH COVID-19 TESTING

One concern is that doctors also still aren't sure what the aftereffects of COVID-19 might be or how it might affect even those without symptoms years down the road. Some children and teens have shown symptoms of an inflammatory disease possibly connected to the virus. Some people have experienced symptoms including shortness of breath, tiredness, and achy joints for months. The virus can also permanently damage the heart, lungs, and brain, although scientists are still studying these long-term effects.

Scientists have rushed to develop treatments and vaccines for COVID-19. Vaccine development usually takes many years, with multiple stages of testing. Before any drug or treatment becomes available in the United States, the U.S. Food and Drug Administration (FDA) must give its approval. Vaccines for COVID-19 were approved on an emergency basis in late 2020, giving hope to billions worldwide. Treatments have also been rapidly developed. Some experimental drugs have failed while others continued to show promise.

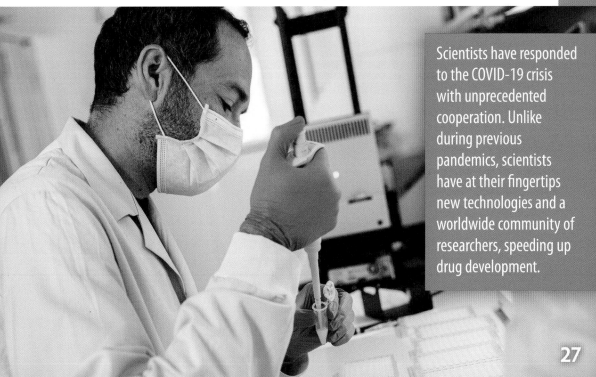

Scientists have responded to the COVID-19 crisis with unprecedented cooperation. Unlike during previous pandemics, scientists have at their fingertips new technologies and a worldwide community of researchers, speeding up drug development.

CHAPTER THIRTEEN

MAKING
A DIFFERENCE

The COVID-19 pandemic has been hard on many people. In addition to the many people who've suffered from the illness and the people who've died or lost loved ones, many people lost their jobs. Some employees had to choose between staying safe and keeping their jobs. When schools shut down, some students lost reliable access to education. Parents had to find ways to keep their kids home and still work. People also had to make decisions about how they were going to react to measures put in place to protect others. Some embraced them. Others were more concerned with personal freedoms.

Many young people have stepped up to make a difference during the pandemic and its many challenges. Avi Schiffmann, a teenager from Washington State, created a COVID-19 tracker online (ncov2019. live/data), one so thorough that scientists have used it. He had help from a team of other teenagers from around the world. Some young journalists joined the Teenage Reporting Project COVID-19 (www. globalyouthandnewsmediaprize.net/project-world-teenage-reporting-pro). The project has included many stories about young people doing their best to make a difference in many ways.

Some young people have found new ways to create equipment to help in the COVID-19 fight. Awuor Onguru, a teenager from Kenya, created face shields for medical workers out of yoga mats. Claire Kang of the United States helped start Washington Youth for Masks to provide safety equipment to hospitals. Other students, such as Brandon Gregory of the United States, have created face masks with 3-D printers.

You don't have to create a website or start an organization to fight COVID-19. The United Nations recommends that young people take measures such as following safety guidelines, educating their friends and family members, and communicating with their government leaders.

BRANDON GREGORY

CHAPTER FOURTEEN

A CHANGED
WORLD

With the rise of COVID-19, the world changed forever. In early October 2020, President Trump was diagnosed with COVID-19—days after he questioned mask use during a presidential debate. The United States continued to have the largest number of cases and deaths in the world. As of late February 2021, there had been more than 28 million cases in the United States, and more than 500,000 Americans had died. Worldwide, there had been more than 113 million cases and more than 2.5 million deaths.

Things are different for everyone. Masks continue to be widespread precautions against the virus. Sporting events may not have live spectators if they're taking place at all. Schools may have all-online classes or hybrid classes that combine online and live classes—or they may be cautiously back to full live classes. Businesses continue to contend with the safety of customers and employees versus making money. The economy is still recovering. No one truly knows just what the future will look like.

Pandemics, from the plagues of the Middle Ages to COVID-19, have always caused great amounts of change in society and history. There may still be quarantines and lockdowns coming. People will have to work together and care about their neighbors to get us all through this time. Young people will step up to make a difference and lead the United States into the future.

There may be changes in health care, education, work, and entertainment. People may have to get creative to meet new needs and concerns. Together, however, we can make it through this and into a post-COVID-19 future.

GLOSSARY

Byzantine Empire (BIH-zuhn-teen EHM-pyr) The eastern half of the Roman Empire, which survived for a thousand years after its fall, and fell in the 1400s.

contradict (kahn-truh-DIKT) To assert the opposite of something.

density (DEHN-suh-tee) The amount of a matter or something else in a given area.

epidemiology (eh-puh-dee-mee-AH-luh-jee) A branch of medical science that deals with disease in a population.

incubation period (in-kyuh-BAY-shuhn PEER-ee-uhd) The period of time after someone has caught a virus, but before it multiplies enough that the person shows symptoms.

individualism (in-duh-VIH-juh-wuh-lih-zuhm) A belief that the needs of each person are more important than the needs of society. Also, an idea stressing the independence of the individual.

inflammatory (in-FLAA-muh-tor-ee) Having to do with a bodily response to injury or disease in which part of the body becomes warm, red, and swollen.

influenza (in-flu-EHN-zuh) A sickness that can include fever, upset stomach, and aches and pains; also known as the flu.

isolate (EYE-suh-layt) To keep apart from others.

pneumonia (new-MOH-nyuh) A serious disease that affects the lungs.

quarantine (KWOHR-uhn-teen) Keeping something away from the public to stop the spread of disease. Also, to keep something away from the public to stop the spread of disease.

sanitation (sa-nuh-TAY-shuhn) The process of keeping places free from dirt and disease.

super-spreader (SOO-puhr–SPREH-duhr) A person who is contagious with a disease and passes it to many other people.

vector (VEK-tohr) A creature that spreads disease from one source to another.

ventilator (VEN-tuh-lay-tuhr) A device that moves air into the lungs of a patient who can't breathe on their own.

INDEX

PRIMARY SOURCE LIST

Page 9
Policemen wearing face masks during the flu epidemic. Photograph. 1918. Seattle, Washington. Held by Time Life Pictures.

Page 11
Portrait of Hippocrates. Painting. ca. 400 BC. Held by Getty Images.

Page 29
Brandon Gregory and face masks he created. Photograph. 2020. Dix Hills, New York. Alejandra Villa Loarca. Held by Getty Images.

WEBSITES

Due to the changing nature of Internet links, Rosen Publishing has developed an online list of websites related to the subject of this book. This site is updated regularly. Please use this link to access the list: www.powerkidslinks.com/SOGI/pandemics